The Herald

J.T. Rumbach
Co-Chairman/Publisher Emeritus

Edwin Rumbach
Co-Chairman/Ad Director

John Rumbach
Co-Publisher/Editor

Dan Rumbach
Co-Publisher/CFO

FRIENDS & NEIGHBORS: A Tribute To The People Of Dubois County ©1994 by The Herald, Jasper, Indiana. All rights reserved. Printed in the United States of America. No part of this book may be used or reproduced in any manner whatsoever without written permission except in the case of reprints in the context of reviews. For information, write The Herald, 216 East Fourth Street, Jasper, IN 47546.

ISBN: 1-884850-05-7

Library of Congress Catalog Card Number: 95-75259

STEVE MELLON

Friends & Neighbors

A Tribute To The People Of Dubois County

The Herald

Edited & Designed By
J. BRUCE BAUMANN

SCRIPPS HOWARD PUBLISHING, INC.

Ethel Nicholson, 95, has been the Cuzco correspondent for The Herald since 1967. She now collects most of her news items for the weekly column over the phone, reporting on who visited whom, who now owns the house on the corner and who died the past week.

This place we call home

IT seemed natural that we'd want to do something special for The Herald's 100th anniversary. So we did.

This is a tribute to the people of Dubois County. This is for all who call this place home.

There are those who say Dubois County is unique and we would agree. The people who live and work here make it that way. They value their families, their work, their religions and their land. They value the youth of the community and the schools that teach them. Many say that's why the county so often excels in business, agriculture, academics, athletics and volunteerism.

So we wanted to publish a book that was as unique as the county, a book that showed the spirit of the people.

We could have produced a history of the county, or a book with pictures from the past, or a book showcasing landscapes and landmarks.

None of these seemed to get to the heart of the county as it is today. We decided, instead, to show people doing what they do every day. We did that by collecting pictures taken by tal-

TIM MYERS

ented Herald photojournalists over the past 15 years. Herald writers researched and wrote about the people and places in the pictures.

You have in your hands the culmination of that work. Unfortunately, we couldn't picture all who made Dubois County what it is. Still, the pictures in the book tell a story. In total, the pictures present a snapshot of the soul of a strong midwestern community.

For 100 years, The Herald has provided daily glimpses of pieces of the county's fabric. This was an opportunity to put together a collection of those pictures that presents a broader view. The book is a reminder that there is much to celebrate here. We're thankful we're part of it.

—*John Rumbach*
Editor, The Herald

MARK T. OSLER

Sometimes the demands of raising a child mount up. While hanging laundry with her 10-year-old granddaughter, Brittany Voelkel, who reeled off her schedule of softball practices and games, Frances Bauer feigned collapse. Brittany — who was not yet 3 when her mother, Kathy, died — has lived with her grandmother ever since. The two share many interests: They watch the same TV programs, they enjoy flea markets and country music, they like to take walks and look at the stars. For three summers, Frances even coached Brittany's softball team. "I never had a chance to be a grandmother," Frances says.

TIM MYERS (Both)

The first extras arriving at Huntingburg League Stadium for the 1991 filming of "A League of Their Own" sat next to plywood cutouts. The wooden people were used whenever an insufficient number of local residents volunteered for the day's filming. Columbia Pictures' makeover specialists gave thousands of local people the '40s look before sending them onto the set and into the past. The hit motion picture helped put Huntingburg on the map. Tourists still visit the stadium to see where Madonna, Tom Hanks and Geena Davis once dug in and took swings of the bat.

When it comes to baseball, there's nothing like starting young. But a plywood backstop isn't a bad idea when new hitters like 4-year-old Troy Leinenbach of Jasper attempt their first swings. Troy's dad, Brad, was on the mound.

Wood in, desks out. Gary Kidwell, a finisher at Jasper Desk, sands and buffs the final finish on desk tops. Jasper Desk was founded in 1876. Dubois County's furniture companies shipped $360 million worth of goods in 1987, the last census of manufacturers. More than 4,000 people work with wood in the county, many from families that have worked wood for generations.

TIM MYERS

Sewing quality leather and cotton gloves is a craft still carried on at the Jasper Glove Co. in Jasper, which celebrated its 75th anniversary in 1994. At its peak in 1944, it employed 170 at its Jasper plant and 46 at its Ferdinand Plant.

STEVE MELLON

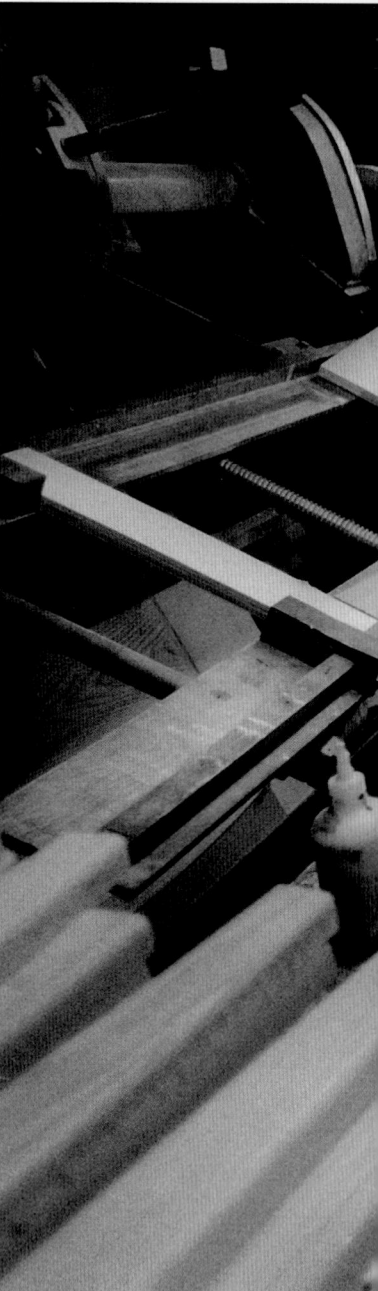

TIM MYERS

Best Chairs in Ferdinand is one of the largest manufacturers of occasional chairs in the world. Workers like Patty Fischer sew fabric for recliners and glide rockers that come in nearly 200,000 different combinations of colors, fabrics and styles. Best Chairs is the third largest furniture company in the county, behind Kimball International and Aristokraft.

TORSTEN KJELLSTRAND

For 31 years, Ed Giesler has made furniture for the Jasper Corporation. Working the glue wheel, a rotating set of clamps, he glues together the top for a television cabinet. In 1950, Arnold Habig bought the financially struggling Midwest Manufacturing, renamed it The Jasper Corporation, and started making television and radio cabinets with about 25 employees. That company grew into the 7,000-employee Kimball International. Today, the Jasper Corporation is part of the contract furniture group of Kimball and still makes television cabinets. Other groups manufacture a variety of products including pianos, office, home and hospitality furniture, electronic components and office systems.

ALAN PETERSIME

Heavy rains in June of 1979 submerged lowland crops in Dubois and surrounding counties. Farmer Oscar Stemle of St. Anthony could only watch as the flood waters covered corn and soybeans. Some farmers gambled and replanted. They lost when another flood swept the bottomlands in July.

ALAN PETERSIME

In 1959, Jasper High School Athletic Director Cabby O'Neill persuaded a raw 21-year-old to become the school's head football coach. Two-hundred and ninety wins later, Jerry Brewer is a coaching legend in Indiana — and one of the area's most colorful sporting personalities. Brewer has taken three teams to the state finals and is Indiana's winningest high school football coach with a 290-87-2 career record. Ever superstitious, Brewer wears the same style hat at all games.

As August temperatures and humidity soar, so does the intensity of two-a-day football practices. Usually lasting two weeks, the purpose of two-a-days is to get the players in shape, develop a cohesive squad and shake off the rust before the first game. Here, Jasper High School senior defensive end Greg Buechlein meets a blocker straight-on during the morning session of a 1985 two-a-day.

STEVE MELLON (Both)

Successful as the Jasper football program has been, the Wildcats have endured their share of disappointments. Here, dejected senior John Sander typifies the feeling in the locker room after Evansville Reitz knocked off sixth-ranked Jasper in the sectional in 1985. Jasper returned the favor the following year, dumping top-ranked Reitz in the sectional in a 10-7 thriller.

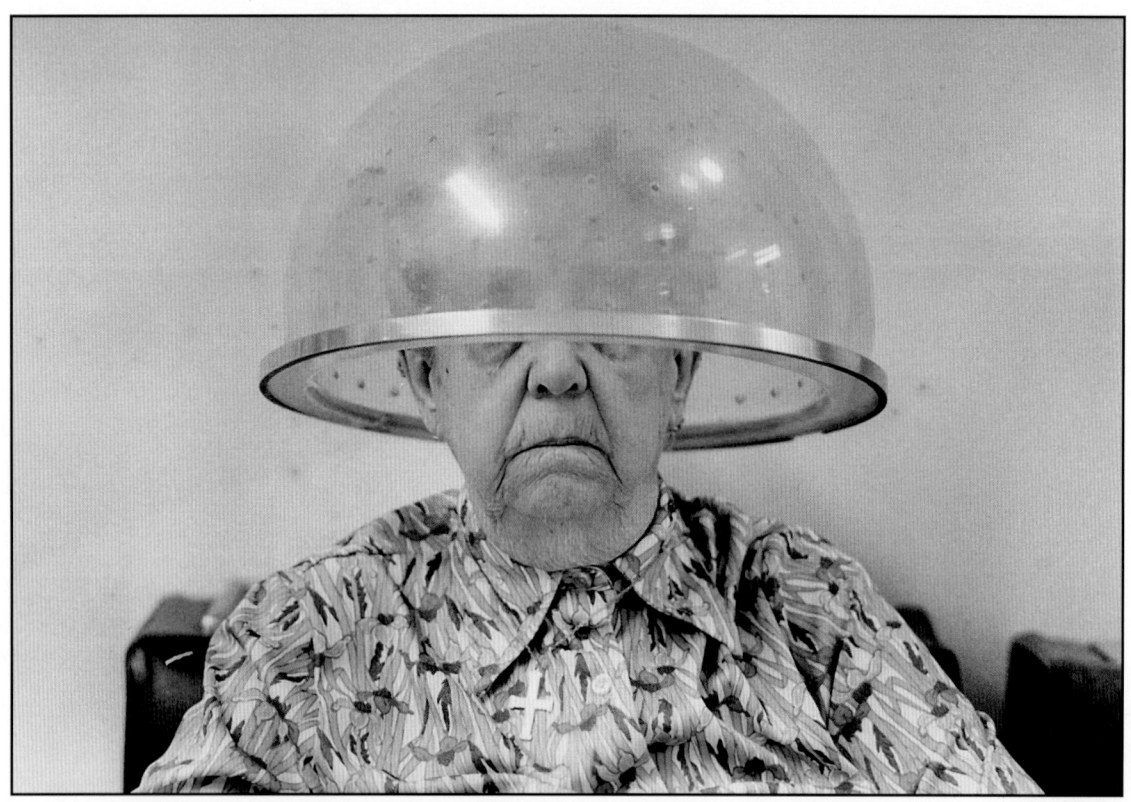

JEFF TUTTLE

𝒞lementine Ellsworth decided to enter the nursing home after a second fall in an apartment where she had lived alone. "I never thought I'd want to go out and live with any of my family, because they have their lives to live." Here, she visits the beauty parlor at the Huntingburg Convalescent Center. A retired teacher who began her career in Huntingburg in 1914, Mrs. Ellsworth died in 1991 at the age of 100.

For Margaret Reyling, the best seat in the house was the soft chair by the dining room window, her crochet hook darting in and out of carefully formed stitches. Mrs. Reyling, who taught herself to crochet as a young girl, spent many an afternoon there, working on afghans. "I'm not so fast with them now, but usually it takes me only about a week to do one," she said a few months before her death in 1984 at the age of 90. A 60-year member of the home economics Achievement Club, Mrs. Reyling also was known for her handmade quilts.

ALAN PETERSIME

Four generations have watched the outside world change through the glass-windowed front of Sturm's Hardware. They've seen the dirt street paved, seen businesses come and go. Inside the store, nothing ever changes, says Sharon Messmer, the late Hugo Sturm's niece. She and her mother, Luella Sturm, moved from clerks to managers when Hugo suffered a stroke in 1983. The 102-year-old hardware has been featured in newspapers and on television, but simple stories don't begin to explain the place. For a century, the same boxes of brackets and screws, the same shovels and rakes have lined the walls; a selection of light bulbs hangs from the ceiling by 50-year-old chains; a carton of wooden canes — just $5 each, your choice — sits in the back of the store. "They always say if you can't find it anywhere else, go to Sturm's," Luella says.

STEVE MELLON

The sun seems to shine a little brighter on the first Saturday in October every year, glinting off trumpets and silken flags of high-school bands competing at District competition in Jasper. Bands start practicing in late summer and hone their skills at contests throughout the fall; it all leads up to District, Regional and State, where the judges' scores are law. Despite all the props they catch and all the notes they hit, bands and color guards seem to remember only the mistakes while they're waiting to hear the results, like Jeana Mathies, right, a member of the Jasper guard who was comforted by Stacey Letterman at the 1993 District. Jeana needn't have worried. The band went on to State. Below, Jasper field commanders Beth Weil, Leslie Krodel and Amanda Miller gaze around the Hoosier Dome before taking the field at the '93 finals.

TIM MYERS

MARK T. OSLER

A long day of tuning up, squeezing in a last-minute practice, performing a six-minute routine and gnashing your teeth while the judges tally score sheets can wear on a band member. Even when a band makes it to the next level of competition, there's always work to be done; using videotapes of the performance and audio tapes recorded by the judges, directors pinpoint weaknesses and keep their students marching double-time to smooth out the rough spots. At the 1986 District contest, Marching Raider Gretchen Gentry, a baritone player, took a break from it all, grabbing a few moments alone in the shadow of the Southridge bus.

STEVE MELLON

At a band contest, the moments before the awards are announced can be agony. Forest Park color guard members, waiting anxiously for the results of the 1993 District competition, had their nervousness relieved by a coveted Division One rating and eventually ended up at the state finals in Indianapolis. Excellence is a tradition with the Marching Rangers, whose history of trips to the state finals is something to envy: 20 of the last 21 seasons have wrapped up with a trip to state. They've won the state four times.

MARK T. OSLER

TIM MYERS

Sgt. Norman Weber of the Indiana State Police knew just how to raise a smile on the faces of Southridge High School athletes gathered for a team picture in March of 1993. Weber, public information officer at the Jasper post, told photographer Marvin Boeglin, "I'll make 'em laugh." Weber started wearing Superman T-shirts 27 years ago. It helped lighten up particularly surly drunks. "I would ask them if they knew who they were messing with. They would just laugh about it." Weber recalls an incident at the state fair: An intoxicated carnival worker climbed a roller coaster, slipped and became wedged in the framework. Weber peeled off his uniform shirt, climbed the coaster, attached the man to himself with his belt and climbed down. Fairgoers cheered wildly at Superman's heroic efforts. "I'll tell you. It makes people remember you."

MARK T. OSLER

When the Emmanuel Evangelic Lutheran Church near Dubois was built in 1901, it was known by its German name, Evangelische Lutherische Emanuels Kirchen. The Victorian Gothic structure, now referred to as "the Hill Church," was included on the National Register of Historic Places in 1990. Jim Keller, below, is one of several people who maintain the property. Other county buildings on the register include Salem Church, the Monastery Immaculate Conception, Lemmon's Church and Cemetery, the Gutzweiler-Gramelspacher House, the Huntingburg Town Hall and Fire Engine House, the Green Tree Hotel or John Opel House and the Shiloh Meeting House.

The four clock faces on St. Joseph Church in Jasper were refurbished in 1990. Clay Jones of Helming Brothers Construction, Jasper, stripped sealant from the metal supports with a blow torch. The church was built by parishioners from 1867 to 1880 under the direction of Fr. Fidelis Maute, O.S.B., who served as architect, contractor, foreman and pastor. The Romanesque structure has sandstone walls 4 to 6 feet thick with a seating capacity of 1200. It was placed on the National Register of Historic Places in 1980.

TIM MYERS (Both)

STEVE MELLON

Priests lined up at the end of vespers March 1, 1987, to greet the newly-installed Bishop of Memphis, the Most Rev. Daniel M. Buechlein. Today, the Jasper native is Archbishop of Indianapolis. For a man who had spent 30 years as a Benedictine monk, the transition to bishop required some adjustments. "I didn't have a checking account. I appeared on the tax rolls for the first time. I'm surprised I didn't get audited. The IRS must have wondered, 'Where did he come from at age 48?'" Now 57, Archbishop Buechlein has never forgotten his origins or the childhood admonition of his late mother, Rose: "Just because you're a leader, don't ever start thinking you're better than anyone you lead."

MARK T. OSLER

Religion is deeply rooted in Dubois County and the devout express their faith in many ways. In some churches, farmers and gardeners gather to pray for their soil, seeds and crops during the annual Rogation Service. Here, Clara Dunn, Rockport, and Hubert Verkamp, Ferdinand, brought seeds to an April, 1993, service led by Bishop Gerald Gettelfinger at St. Ferdinand Catholic Church. Rogation services date back to the early Catholic Church.

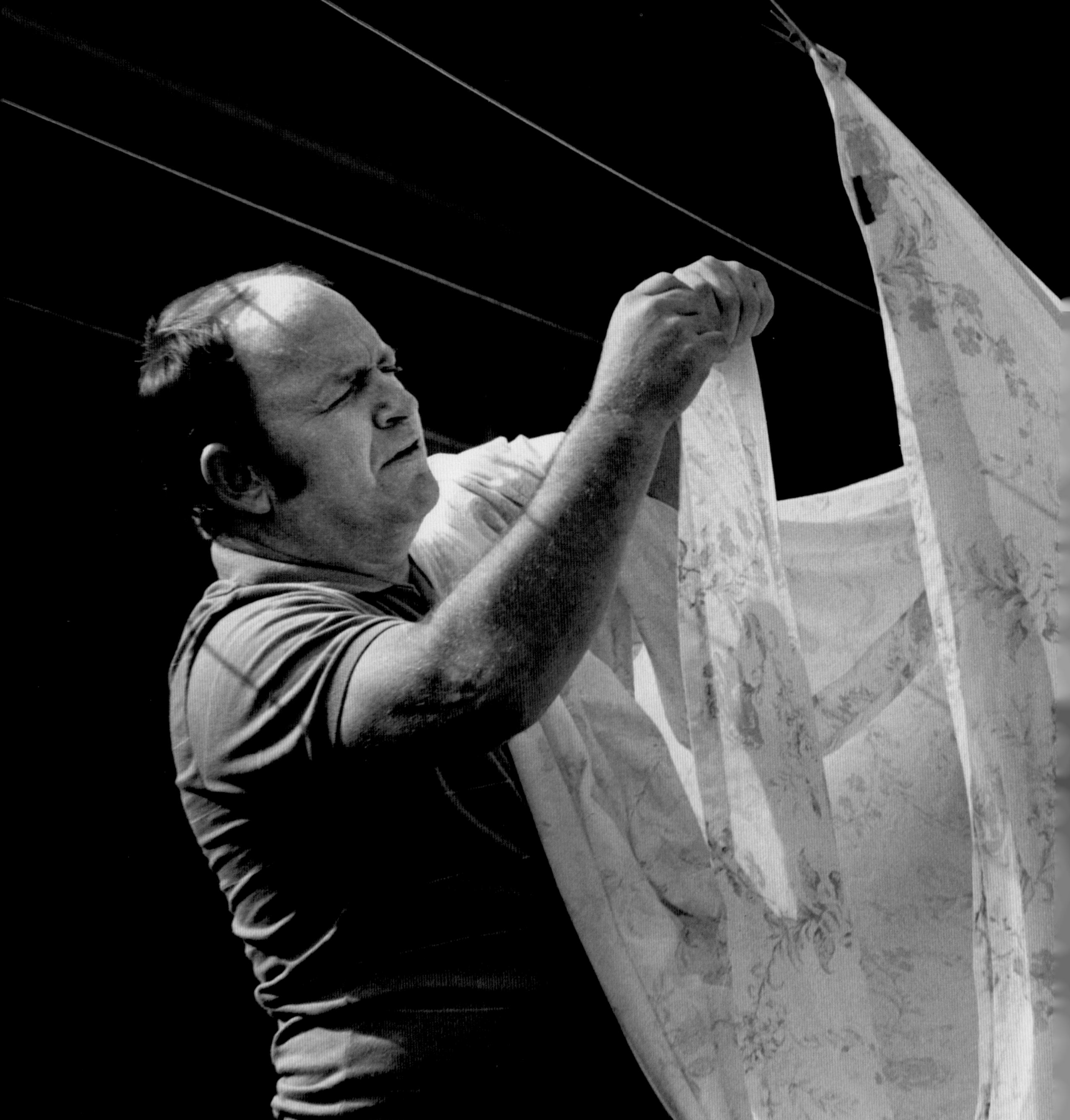

Blinded in a 1971 automobile accident, David Recker of St. Anthony was determined to live life to the fullest. His full-speed-ahead approach has not been without peril. Like the time he knocked an out building off its foundation while attempting to drive a tractor. Or the time he mistook a 10-foot drop-off for a 5-inch snow-covered step leading to his basement door. Or the time he singed his hair when the food he was grilling caught on fire. Mishaps aside, he's accomplished much. "David's exceptional with blindness," says Beatrice, his wife. "I used to worry, but I don't anymore." Recker says he's learned more about living and how to live life since he was blinded. "I figure it's all a miracle that I'm doing what I'm doing."

STEVE MELLON

The German immigrants who settled in Dubois County brought with them German lore about the moon and its influence on plants, people and things. Lunar signs prescribe when it's best to plant, to roof and even to have surgery. The moon also affects behavior, it's said. Ask the Dubois County sheriff and he'll tell you, "Full moon, full jail."

Not too long ago, hog butchering was a family ritual. In 1988, the German Club met at the Leonard and Viola Wehr farm near Ireland to relive those times. Two hogs were butchered in the tool shed, their heat sending waves of steam against the biting January cold. Club members made whole hog, liver and blood sausages and head cheese and dined on ribs, sauerkraut and mashed potatoes.

ALAN PETERSIME

JEFF TUTTLE

JEFF TUTTLE

Alvin C. Ruxer, one of Indiana's most famous entrepreneurs, called it the "smell of money." He followed its scent to Jasper in 1936 when he opened his Ford dealership. Over the years, he added the Jasper Engine and Transmission Exchange, Ruxer Farms and Jasper State Bank to his long list of successful enterprises. Ruxer, who died in 1991 at age 82, attributed his success to thinking differently, working harder and always being dedicated to the community and its people. As famous for his philanthropy as for his business savvy, he was a force behind the establishment of Vincennes University Jasper Center and gave generously to the school, the St. Meinrad Archabbey and Memorial Hospital as well as community baseball, the sport that was his lifelong love.

TIM MYERS

A concert pianist he's not. But as the founder of Kimball International, Arnold Habig might be a concert pianist's best friend. The boy who delivered newspapers, shined shoes and ushered movie goers became the man who helped turn a floundering manufacturing company into a Fortune 500 firm. People, he always said, were his first concern "because no matter how much brick and mortar you have, if you do not have the personnel, you can't make a success of it." Because of the importance he places on education, college students and learning institutions have benefited most from his philanthropy. Early on, Habig decided to make his company a family enterprise. He is most proud of how his sons — Tom, John and Doug — worked together, and credits them with Kimball's inclusion on Fortune Magazine's list, which it first made in 1988.

TIM MYERS

TIM MYERS

*A*ntique farm machinery demonstrations, held at least once a summer, remind the county of its agricultural heritage. In 1993, Celestine's Sesquicentennial celebration included a threshing display. At right, Brian Beckman tosses wheat into the thresher which Ottie Betz, wiping July sweat and wheat stubble from his face, stands atop. Above, Francis "Franz" Lindauer of Ferdinand collects and restores steam-powered farm equipment, particularly Kitten tractors, with the help of his sons. Kitten tractors were made in Ferdinand from 1880 to 1940. The Lindauers are one of several area families who belong to the Early Days Antique Club.

MARK T. OSLER

It took a little work, but Wesley Gutgsell, 7, kept his cow in line as he prepared for judging in the Pre 4-H class in the 4-H Beef Show. The annual fair lets farm 4-Hers show off their livestock. Animal judging, however, is only one facet of the ever-growing 4-H program. Hundreds of projects, from photography to woodworking, are displayed and judged at the fair.

TRACY L. ALBANO

MARK T. OSLER

It's no wonder an exhausted Matt Steckler of Ferdinand napped after the swine show competition at the 1994 Dubois County 4-H Fair. Many 4-Hers spend a good portion of the week on the fairgrounds taking care of their animals, staying up late, playing basketball and volleyball, sleeping in the barns and showering in the bathrooms.

Slow afternoons at the 4-H Fair sometimes lead to some good-natured goofing around. Tiffany Small and Natalie Ruhe couldn't resist the temptation during the 1989 fair. More than 1,000 Dubois County adults, children and teenagers took part in 4-H in 1994. It takes the 4-H organization a full year of planning and work to pull off the popular county fair.

TIM MYERS

From its two-tabled barroom to its ancient Coca Cola signs, Miller's Restaurant & Bar in Celestine changed little in three quarters of a century. In the summer of 1988, Marie Miller Wehr, right, still owned and operated the grocery store, gas station and bar that her father, Henry K. Miller, built in 1912 as a blacksmith shop, wagon shop and home. The gas station was added in 1917 and a restaurant and bar in the early '30s. With the help of friends and neighbors, Mrs. Wehr kept the business going into her 80s. "I believe I'm going to stick with it until they put me up on the hill," she said, laughing. "This is a landmark. We worked too hard for this place." Mrs. Wehr died in 1991 at the age of 83.

JEFF TUTTLE

STEVE MELLON

Duck hunters from Dubois County were out early this cold November morning in 1988 at Glendale's Himsel Marsh, a 200-acre slough in nearby Daviess County. Hunters say the best time to hunt ducks is on windy, cloudy days when temperatures hover near freezing because ducks have little reason to move on mild, sunny days.

The fish in Izaak Walton Lake were having more luck than Nicole Link who repeatedly lifted her line from the water only to find the bait gone. Nicole was fishing with her friend, Cameron Betz, at the Jasper Outdoor Recreation Center.

MARK T. OSLER

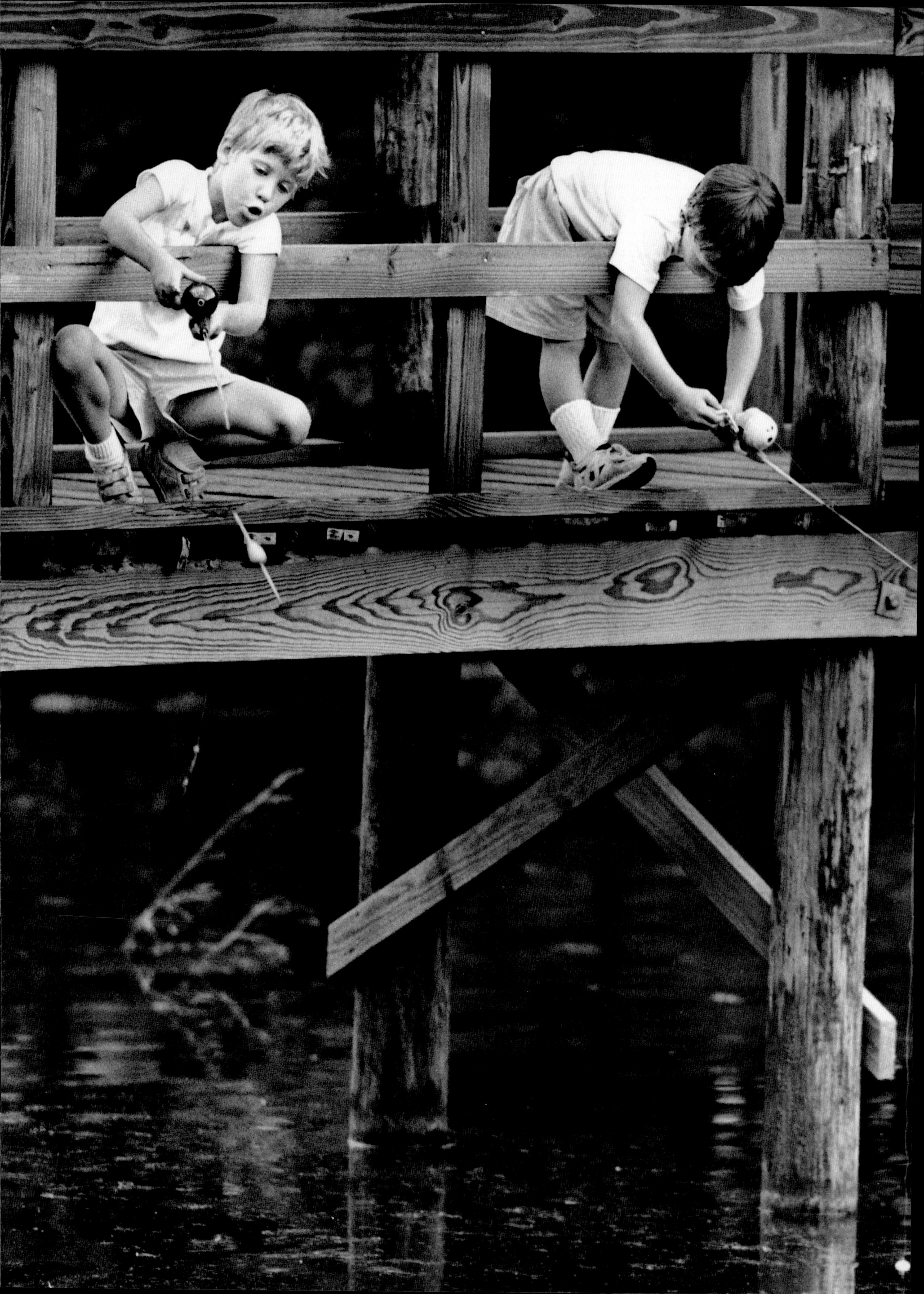

Sultry summer days in southern Indiana sap energy from gardens and 15-year-old boys alike. Scott Prechtel of Jasper found it easier to water his family's garden from the comfort of a lawn chair one hot July day in 1984. Gardens are popular in the county and families pass horticultural advice — rooted in science and German lore — from generation to generation.

ALAN PETERSIME

Edwin Schneider of Jasper wore a sergeant's uniform in the 16th Infantry, U.S. Army 1st Division, during World War II. Schneider was in the first wave of the invasion of Normandy, June 6, 1944. His unit's target: Omaha Beach, scene of the bloodiest fighting of D-Day. Fifty years removed from the nightmarish chaos and carnage of the day, Schneider's voice cracks with emotion as he recalls trying to aid the wounded. "The hardest work was pulling guys out of the way on the beach to let the tanks come in. Many did not get out of the way of our tanks. We were on the beach — about 50 feet in — until noon, pulling out wounded and dead. One died in my arms."

Dan Renneisen was sports editor of The Herald, then a weekly, when he made local history: When the U.S. started its first-ever peace-time draft, Renneisen was the first man from Dubois County to get the call, and among the first draftees nationwide. That was in the fall of 1940, the final year of peace for the U.S. before it entered World War II. Army life appealed to the Jasper native. When the war ended, he stayed in, rising from private to colonel in a 35-year career, much of it in the military intelligence field. After his retirement, he returned to the city of his birth.

The clang of horseshoes hitting stakes is often heard in Ferdinand's 18th Street Park. Here, Dean Zoglman, Ferdinand, tunes up for the summer horseshoe leagues at nearby St. Meinrad. Fairs and fests held throughout the summer and fall usually include horseshoe pitching contests.

MARK T. OSLER

STEVE MELLON

Every once in a while, Henry Hubert would take a break from hoeing, but not this day in 1986. He was 81. He lived a lifetime on rural southern Indiana farms. So did his wife, Blaudina. Together they bought a 100-acre spread in Holland in 1938. They were married 59 years. Henry died in 1988 and Blaudina in 1993.

TIM MYERS

Robert Beck is retired, but he still makes the rounds on his farm southwest of Jasper. Beck, 73 in 1992, claimed he wanted to break in his pony, Charlie, so he could ride him to the nearby Double R Bar. He never made the trip. Charlie, he said, had a wild streak and wouldn't be ridden.

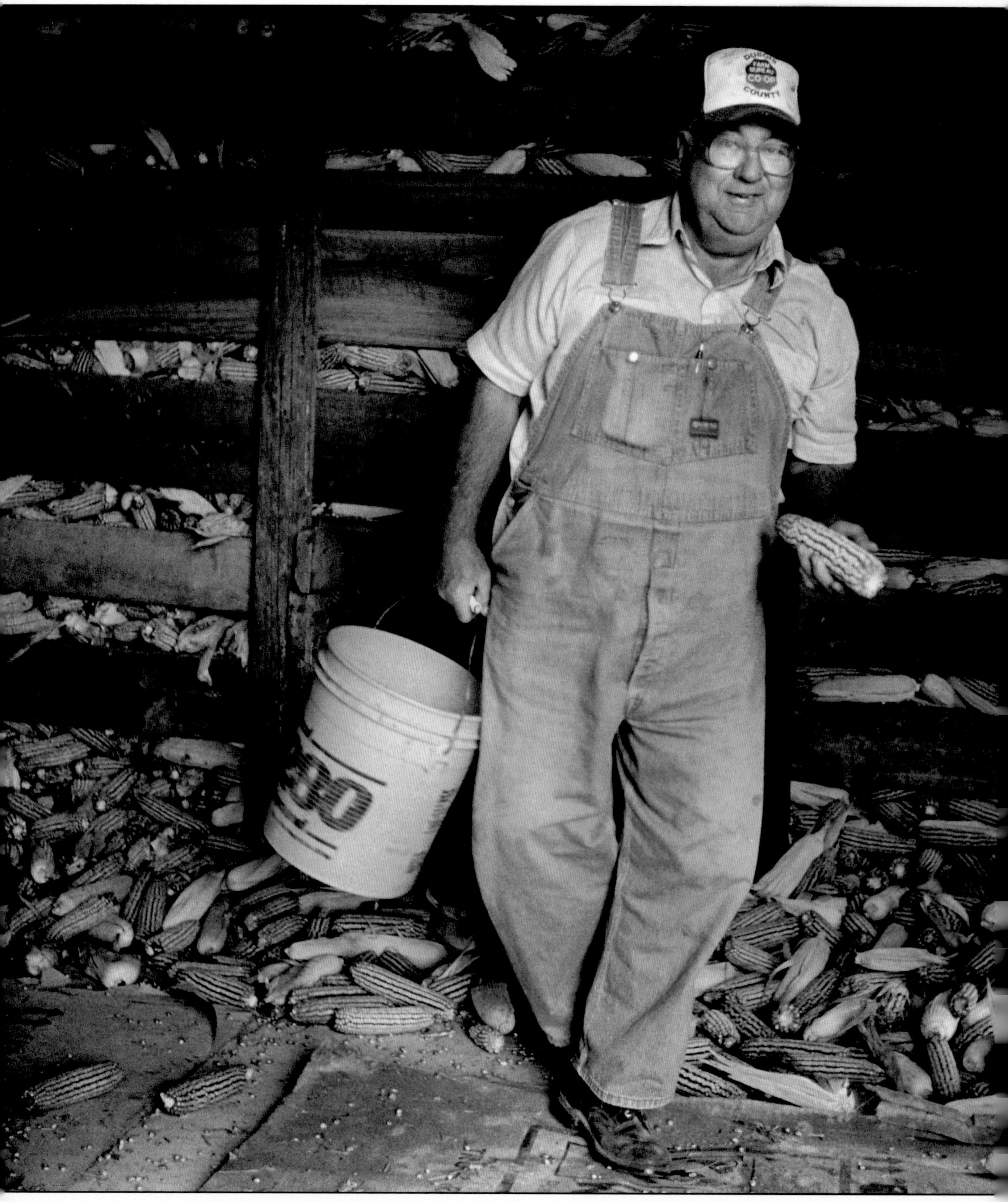
CO-OP
COUNTY

Life-long Birdseye farmer George Hoffman, like all pork producers, has learned to cope with low prices for hogs, high prices for feed, summer droughts and wet harvest seasons. Today, after a couple of bypass surgeries, Hoffman, 67, lets a son do most of the farming in the second holler north of where County Road 1025E meets the Birdseye-Schnellville Road.

TIM MYERS

Bill and Margaret Schroeder visited with family, friends and neighbors who gathered outside their house in Jasper in August of 1985 to welcome Bill home for the first time since an artificial heart was implanted in his chest on Nov. 25, 1984. Some 15,000 people lined the streets later in the day to greet him as he rode in the Strassenfest parade; his surgeon, Dr. William DeVries, was the grand marshal. It was Schroeder's only trip home. He died Aug. 6, 1986. Despite numerous complications and setbacks, Schroeder became the world's longest-living recipient of an artificial heart. How will his contribution ultimately be regarded? "Legacies are determined by people other than the immediate family," Mel Schroeder said, 10 years after his father's historic operation. "He was just my dad. I was proud to call him my dad. That was plenty."

STEVE MELLON (Both)

Burl Ives, Colonel Sanders and Santa Claus rolled into one, with a dash of the mischievous Puck added for good measure, Dr. St. John Lukemeyer and his ever-present cigar were community legends for the 63 years he practiced medicine in Jasper. Jovial and caring, a spinner of yarns and a renowned practical joker, Doc shared his stories for the price of his diagnosis. When he began practicing medicine in the early 1920s, he delivered babies on his portable delivery table and performed appendectomies in country kitchens. During World War II, he kept office hours from 8 a.m. to 9 p.m., then made house calls. He died in 1989 at the age of 91.

WELCOME HOME

STEVE MELLON

Though duck hunting is not as popular as other outdoor pursuits, some hunters like Eric Olinger are willing to sit and wait among the cattails on cold, pre-dawn mornings. Waterfowl are one of the many game species hunted in the area. Others include deer, rabbits, squirrels, wild turkeys, quail and raccoons.

64

MARK T. OSLER

Searching for bargains at garage sales and auctions is popular. On any given summer weekend, you can find dozens of sales. Here, Rose Hughes holds a Model 12 Winchester rifle that she and her husband, Jim, purchased at an auction at the Jasper Armory.

After decades of doing the public's business in cramped offices, Jasper built a new city hall. The lobby, mayor's office and council chamber are finished in a rich cherry stain. The other offices are done in medium oak. A wide staircase curves up from the lobby to the second floor. The 30,000 square foot, $2.5 million city hall was opened in November of 1993.

TIM MYERS

Huntingburg built a new city hall in 1995 and Jasper built one in 1993, but the seat of county government still wants for a facelift. Built in 1910 and remodeled in 1927, the Dubois County courthouse, despite its age, continues to be the hub of county government as witnessed in this photograph, right, taken on general election day in 1982. Another remodeling is planned for the landmark structure. The courthouse sits in the middle of Jasper's town square.

ALAN PETERSIME

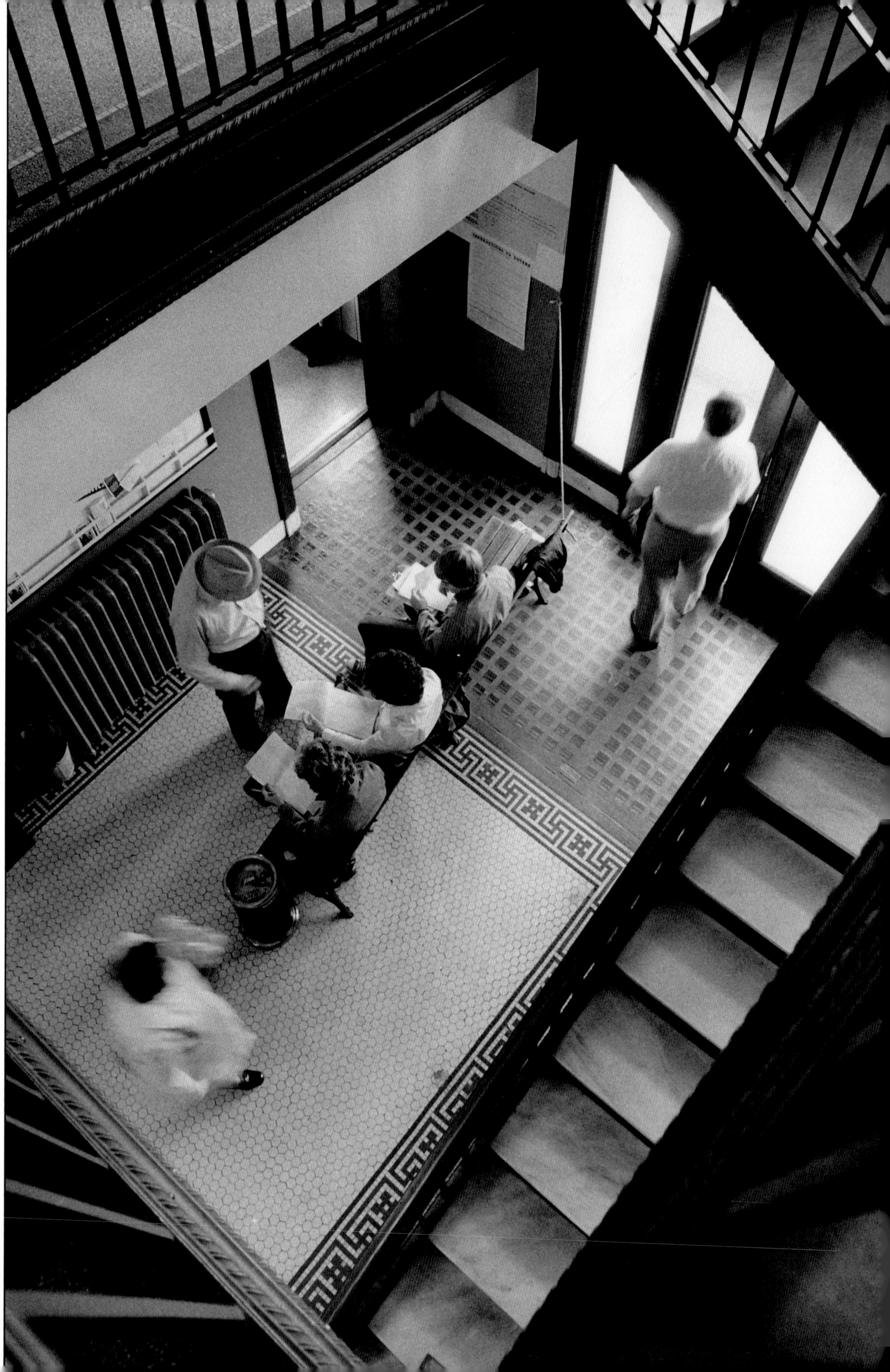

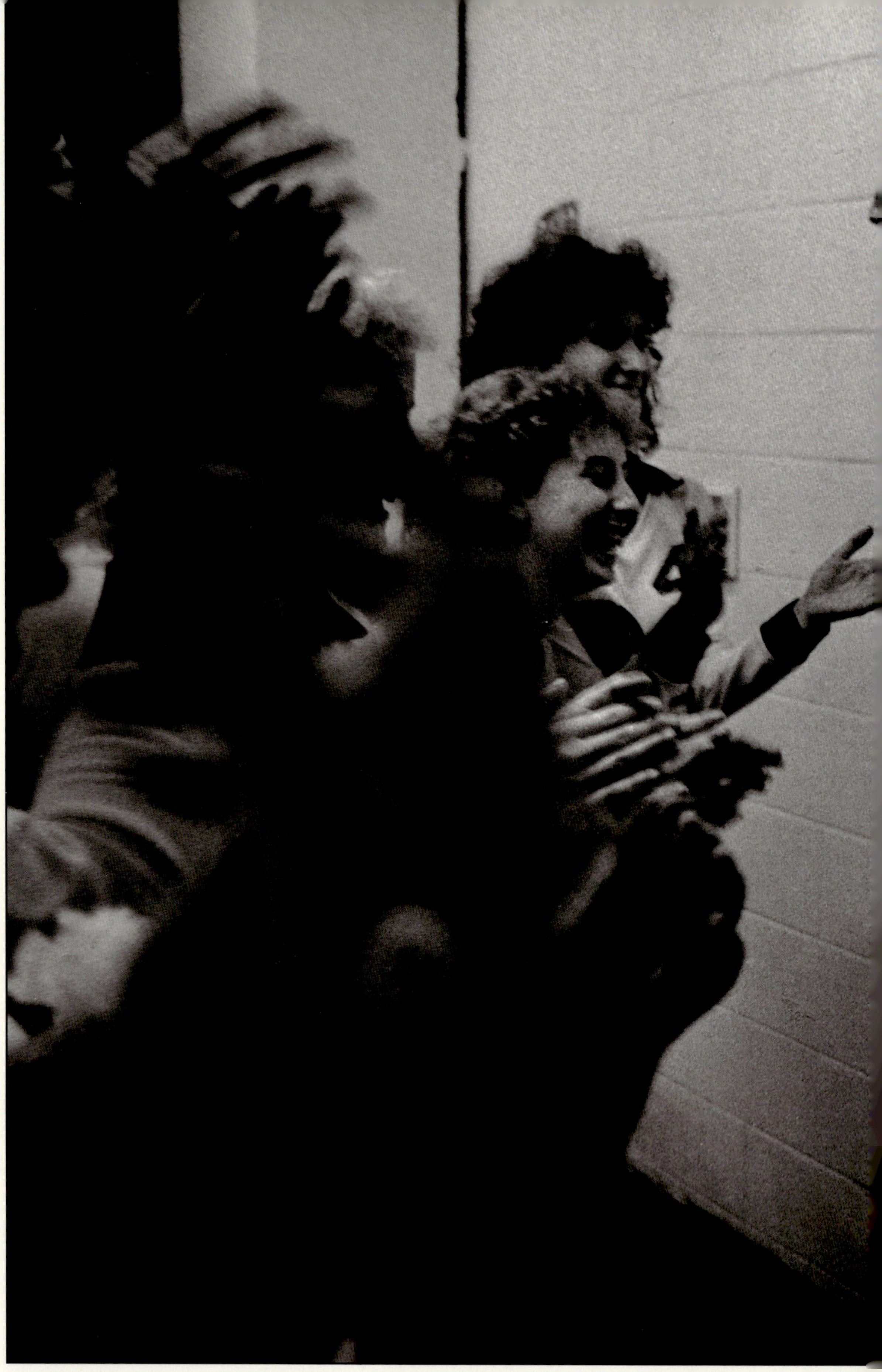

In 1984, Jasper volleyball coach Pat Zehr was tossed into the showers after the Wildcats won the regional, above. It was an often-repeated scene through the years. On Oct. 13, 1994, Zehr was tossed into the showers again, this time following her 500th coaching victory. Zehr's resume at Jasper High School lists 18 sectional titles, 10 regionals, three semistates and a state runner-up.

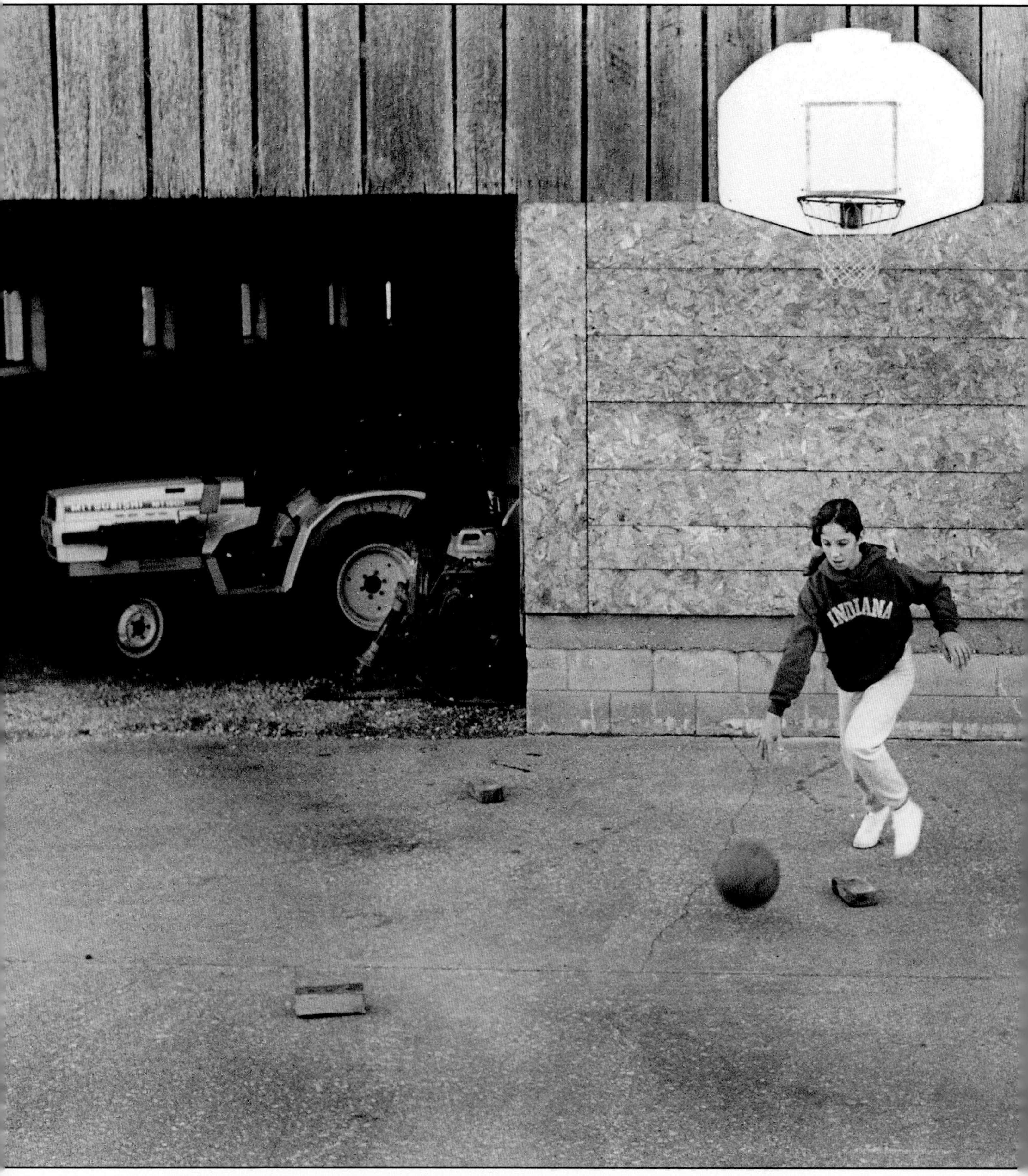
INDIANA

Like every other kid in Indiana, Jessica Schmitt of Ireland wants to become a basketball player. But she knows it takes practice to live that dream — and a little innovation when there aren't real defenders to dribble around. In Dubois County, basketball goals in backyards, barnyards and driveways are as common as garages.

TIM MYERS

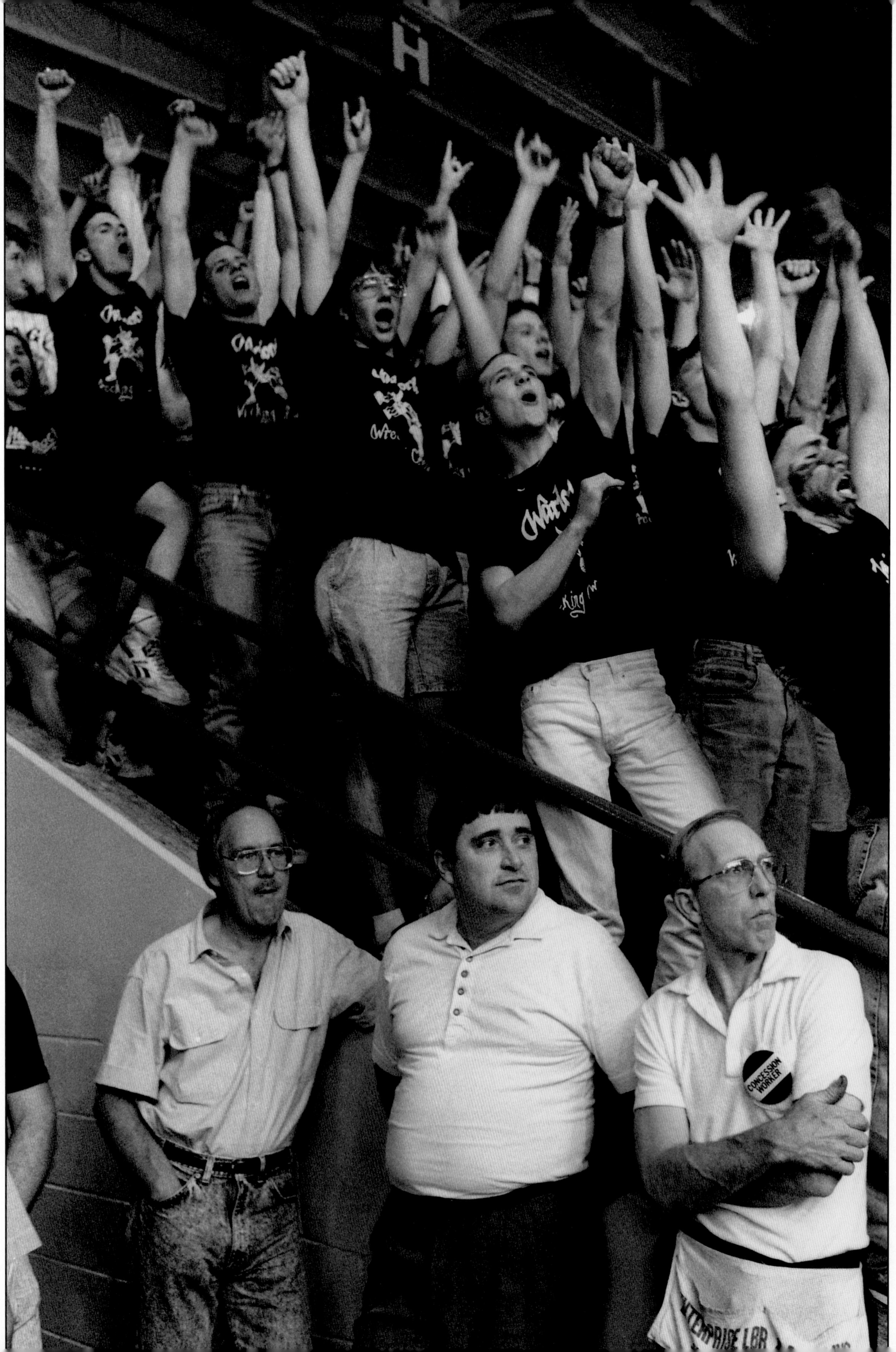
H
CONCESSION WORKER

TIM MYER (Left page and above)

Basketball fever reaches its peak in Dubois County during the opening round of Hoosier Hysteria. At far left, in contrast to the Jasper High School student section, Kevin "Slim" Werne, Gerry Howard and Clyde Kissling quietly watch 1992 Southridge Sectional action from the tunnel leading to locker rooms at Huntingburg's Memorial Gym. At left, Jasper senior John Bottorff celebrates after cutting a piece of the net following the Wildcats' sectional win in 1989. Basketball contests are often part of other events. Above, Reece and Stephanie Van Winkle attempt a fast break toward the court while watching their father play in the Ferdinand Sesquicentennial's 3-on-3 basketball tournament in 1990. Their mother, Rhonda, and Lydia Blessinger pulled the youngsters back to the bench.

JEFF TUTTLE

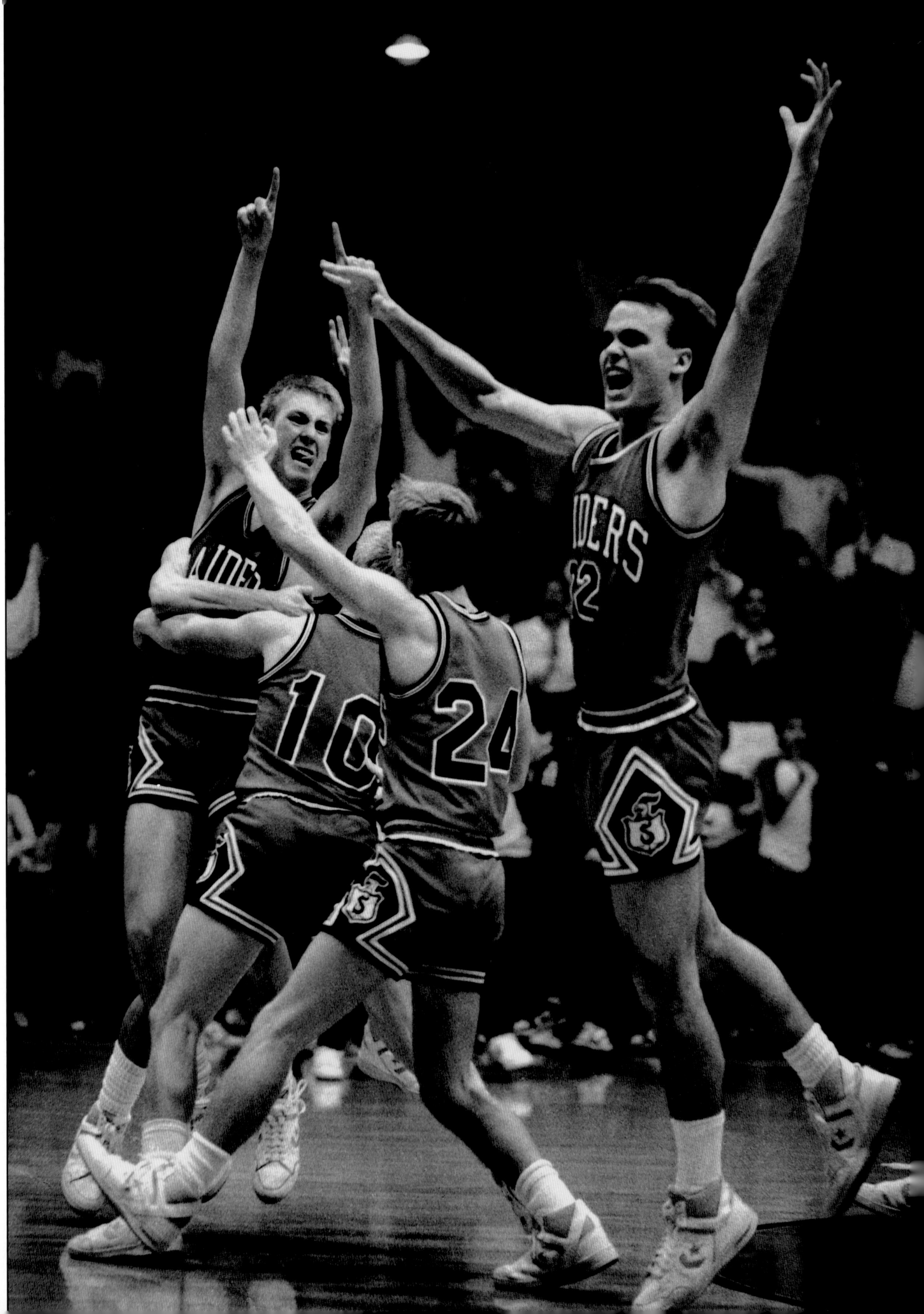
IDERS
24

The 1980s belonged to the Southridge Raiders and head coach Gary Duncan. The Raiders won the sectional six times in 10 years. The team did the impossible two years in a row by advancing to the state finals in '85 and '86. At bottom, Duncan embraces his mother and brother, Roger, following the Raiders' semistate championship in 1985. When Southridge won the sectional in 1987, at left, it became the only other school besides Huntingburg and Jasper to take three crowns in a row. Below, the Raiders also took their knocks when Northeast Dubois defeated them in the final game of the 1982 Holiday Tourney.

ALAN PETERSIME

STEVE MELLON (2)

The signs in the taverns in Ferdinand read, "Doutaz For President," after Forest Park High School coach Denny Doutaz guided the Rangers to their first-ever boys' basketball sectional title on March 5, 1990. The victory sparked a celebration that lasted into the wee hours of the morning. Before the street festivities began, fans gathered at the high school where Doutaz led the 1,300 faithful in the refrain of "Na-Ha, Hey-Hey, Goodbye."

JEFF TUTTLE

Former Birdseye Yellowjacket John Sinclair, who played in the 1917 sectional, was the oldest participant in the Nostalgia Basketball Sectional held in Memorial Gym in Huntingburg in 1989. He still lives in Birdseye. John Small, on the other hand, had to take a week off work and drive from Florida to play in the game. A starting guard for Ireland High School in 1963, Small remembers Ireland's sectional title and the celebration that followed. "The streets flowed with green beer."

TIM MYERS

77

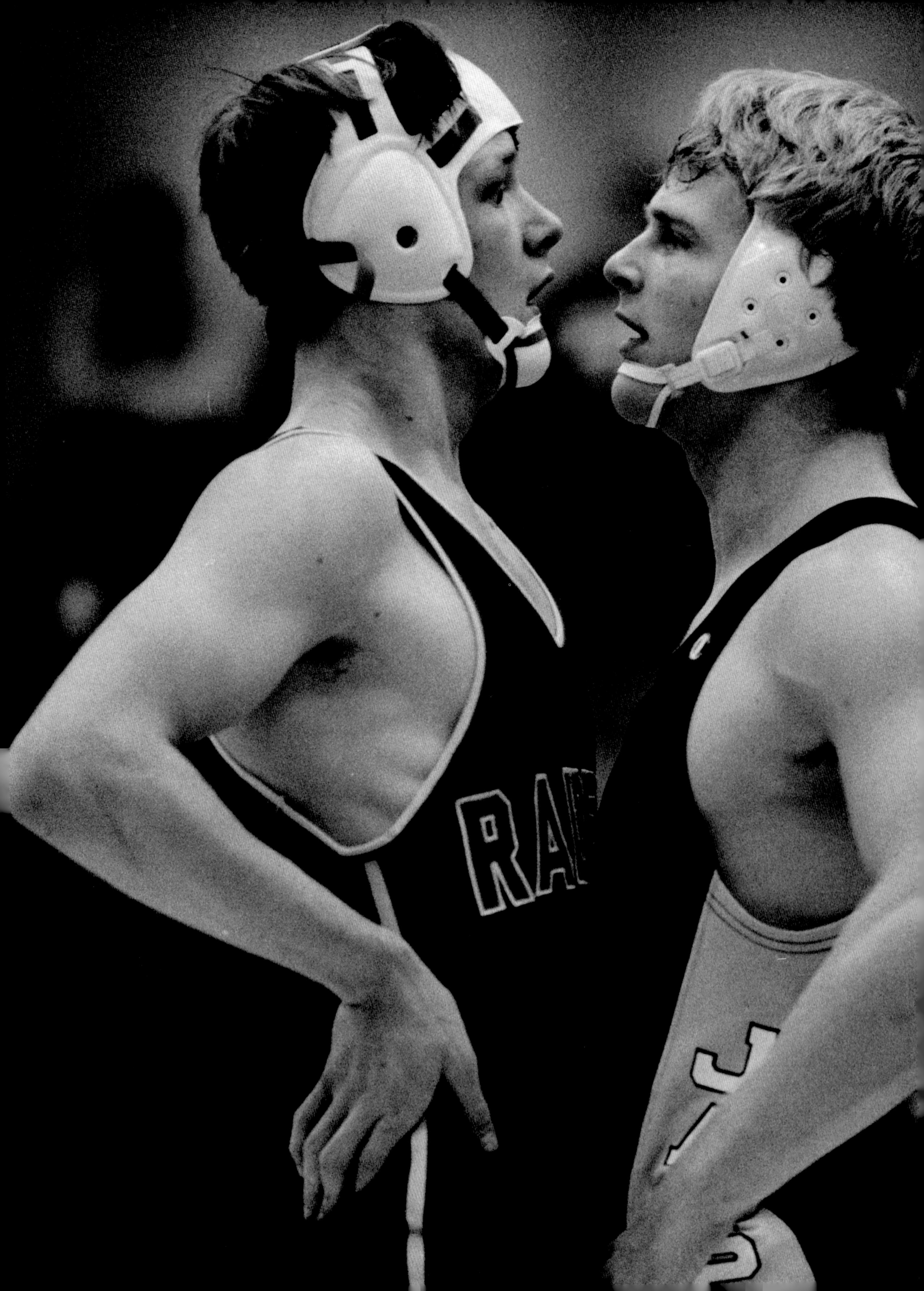

Strong intra-county competition in high school sports has spawned fierce rivalries among schools and their athletes. With their 1984 wrestling sectional championship match finished, Southridge's Scott Proffitt, left, and Jasper's Nick Eckert exchanged a few words. Eckert decisioned Proffitt 13-9 in the 177-pound division that year.

ALAN PETERSIME

JEFF TUTTLE

How strong are county rivalries? Strong enough that for two straight years (1989 and 1990) the Southridge Lettermen's Club hosted a Nostalgia Basketball Sectional where players from the past would don their old uniforms. More than 10,000 fans came out each of the two years to watch. Participants had to have been graduated by 1968. Holland won the Nostalgia title both years and one of the reasons was Don Buse, above. Buse, a 1968 graduate, played professionally in the now defunct ABA, and later in the NBA. A few years after his retirement from the pros, he helped coach Southridge's boys' basketball team.

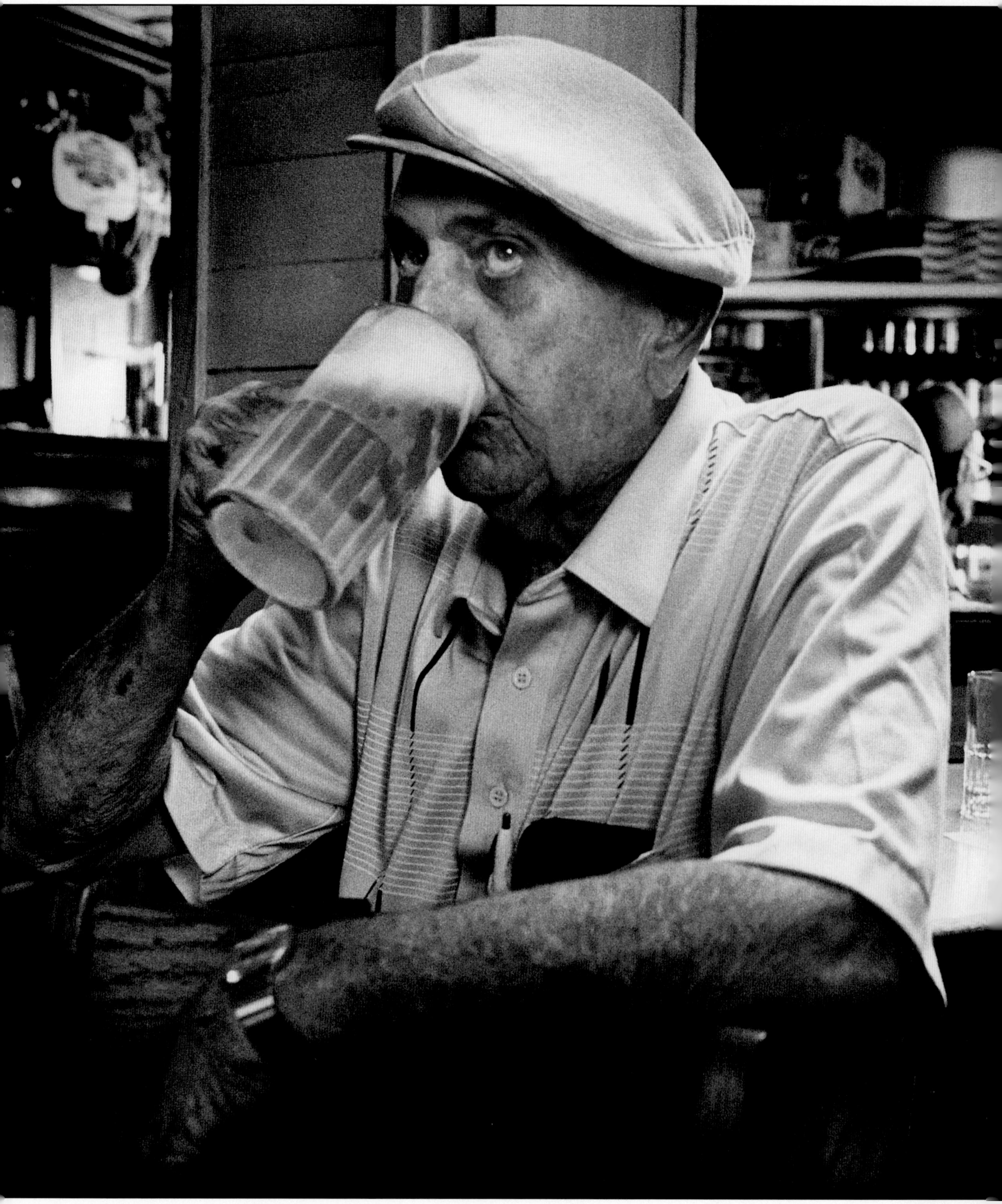

Butchie's Tavern in Dubois was one of many old watering holes that dot Dubois County's landscape. Ralph Terwiske, left, ran a general store in the building, which over the years also housed barbershops, restaurants, a feed mill, a hotel, apartments, and a poultry and egg market. Ralph's son, Butchie, opened the tavern when he was 20, hiring an older bartender until he turned 21. A new building, made from Dubois County-grown tulip poplar, was built next to the old structure in 1989.

TIM MYERS

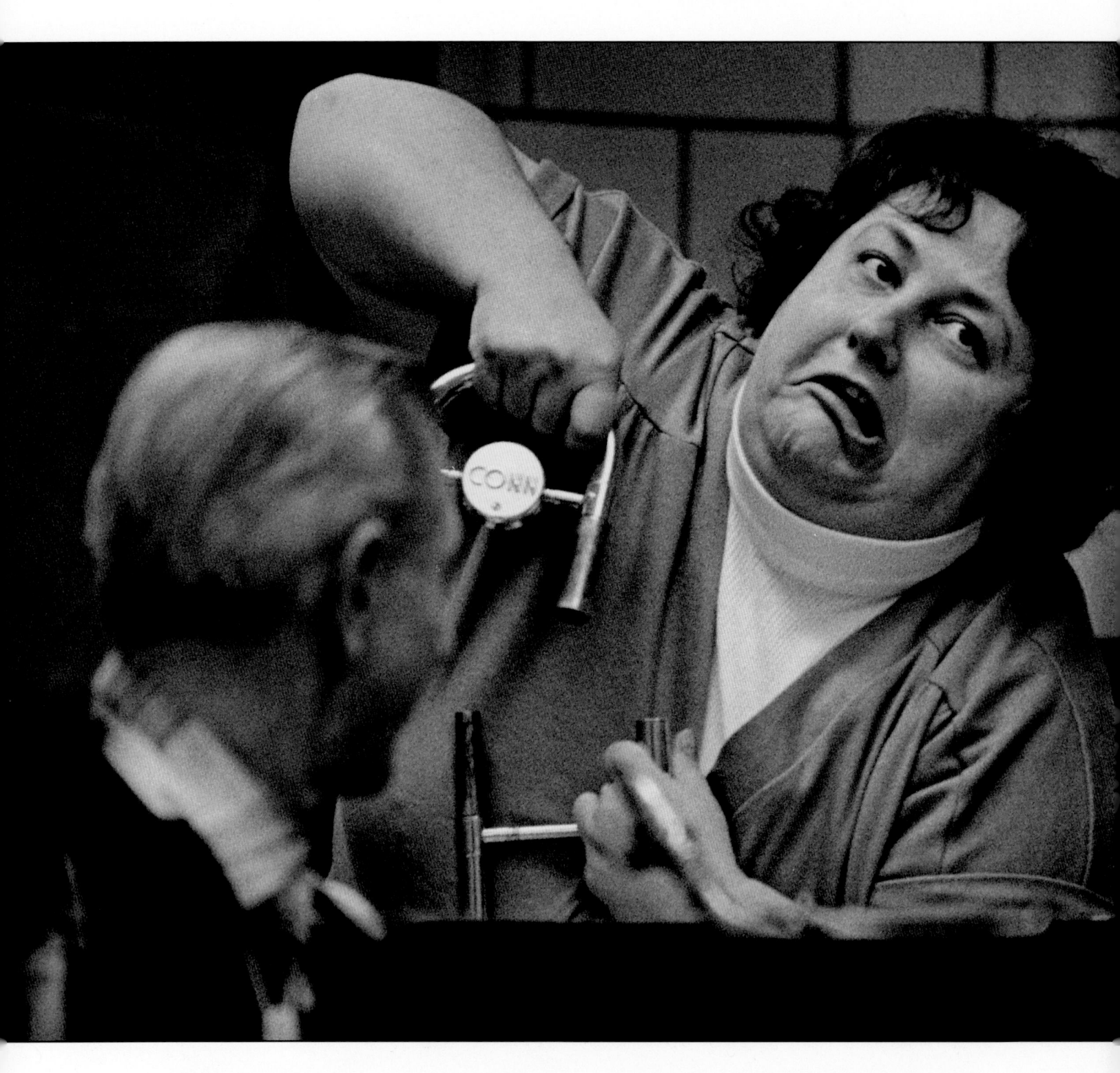

Ruth Helzerman jokes about her used, and sticky, trombone during a 1981 rehearsal of the Dubois County Civic Orchestra. The orchestra, formed in 1974, disbanded in the early 1980's following the death of its director, Art Stillwell. The arts remain a solid fixture in the county. In 1987, Jasper was recognized with the Governor's Arts Award for its strong municipal support of the arts.

Mayor Bill Schmitt fielded some tough questions when third graders from Tenth Street School toured Jasper's new city offices in May of 1994. What exactly do you do? How much do you make? Do you have a big house with a pool? Lindsey Gates, right, couldn't wait to ask a question. Janelle Spellmeyer is in the foreground and Aimee Keusch is in the background.

ALAN PETERSIME

MARK T. OSLER

What *started out as small talk during an annual employee appreciation night hosted by the medical staff at St. Joseph's Hospital turned into tradition after Dr. Tom Field and his wife, Tammy, offered three free lessons in country and western dancing to anyone who was interested. The result? The Silver Spur Dancers who demonstrate line dancing at area festivals, entertain at other events when asked and often get together for some old-fashioned foot stomping at the YMI in Huntingburg.*

TIM MYERS

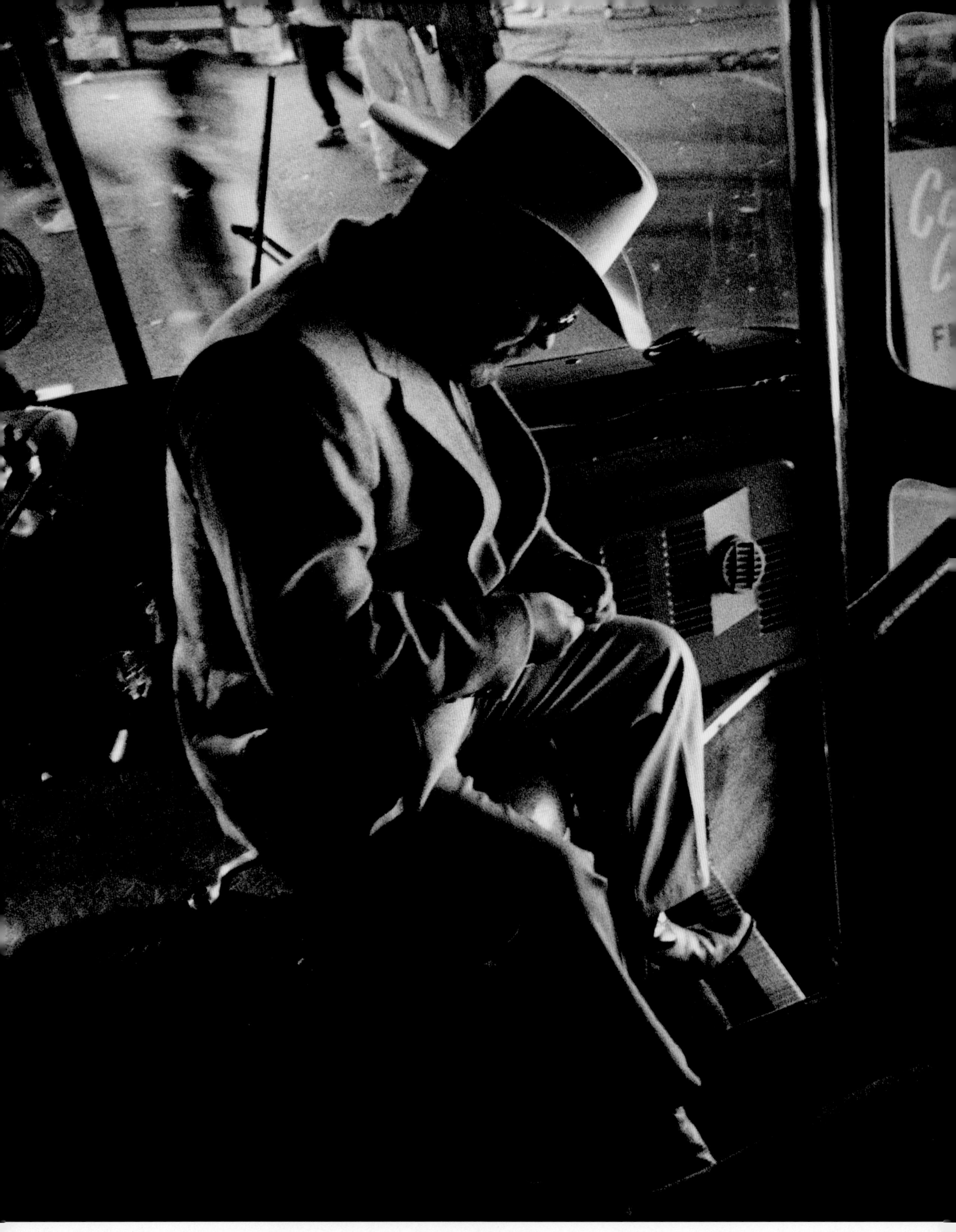

Bill Mounts is the family patriarch of the Midwest Cowboys band comprised of himself and his sons. The musical Huntingburg clan has played western swing alongside the likes of Sweethearts of the Rodeo, Johnny Paycheck, Sylvia and Porter Wagoner. The five-piece band is the star of its own newsletter, record company and promotions firm.

TIM MYERS

TIM MYERS

It's easy to find a celebration in the area on July 4th. The Miss and Little Miss Firecracker Pageants highlight Otwell's festivities. Here, 4-year-old Erin Wehr of Ireland waits for the start of the 1990 Little Miss contest.

The beef at the Dubois County 4-H Fair isn't always found in the livestock arena, especially when men turn into boys, dig their heels into the ground and latch onto a rope. Above, Sara Steckler, Ferdinand, yells at her boyfriend, Brian Betz, during the 1994 tug-of-war. Betz and his Schnellville Tuggers struggled for almost three minutes before a St. Henry team overpowered them.

MARK T. OSLER

TORSTEN KJELLSTRAND

A simple dab of petroleum jelly on the teeth brightened the smile of Julie Linette as she and Angela Mendel prepared for the formal wear competition in the 1993 Strassenfest Queen Pageant.

MARK T. OSLER

Teenagers try on elegance for the first time at high school proms. Here, Holly Reinhart and junior class president Zeke Ziliak circle the dance floor during Jasper High School's "One Enchanted Evening" in 1993.

The movie "American Graffiti" made cruising famous, but most teens who drive the whip in Jasper on warm summer nights would probably swear they invented it. What's up, where's it at, how's it going, who's out tonight, they ask from car window to car window. It's like a grapevine that never ends, unless the cops break it up. Some fast-food restaurants in town hire security guards on the weekends, "human speed bumps" they're called by the cruising kids. Why do they cruise? Anyone who has cruised, from the bobby-soxers of the '50s to the jeans-clad teens of today, can tell you: There's nothing else to do. The joke in Jasper is that you'd be rich if you bought a parking lot and charged teenagers to hang out there.

STEVE MELLON

Forest Park's Karen Braunecker experienced the agony of defeat while watching Evansville Central's victorious 400-meter relay team celebrate at the 1986 girls' track regional. Forest Park's star sprinter, Ann Schwoeppe, who went on to run at the University of Wisconsin, won the 400-meter dash and was state champion in the 100- and 200-meter dashes as a freshman in 1983.

Southridge built a strong girls' track tradition with athletes like Heather Blackgrove, right.

STEVE MELLON

MARK T. OSLER

Hours of practice at his family's backyard pole vault pit in Holland got Mark Buse what he always dreamed of — an NCAA national championship. The Indiana University pole vaulter and former Southridge High School star cleared 18 feet, 4 1/2 inches to earn the title during his sophomore year at IU in 1993.

STEVE MELLON

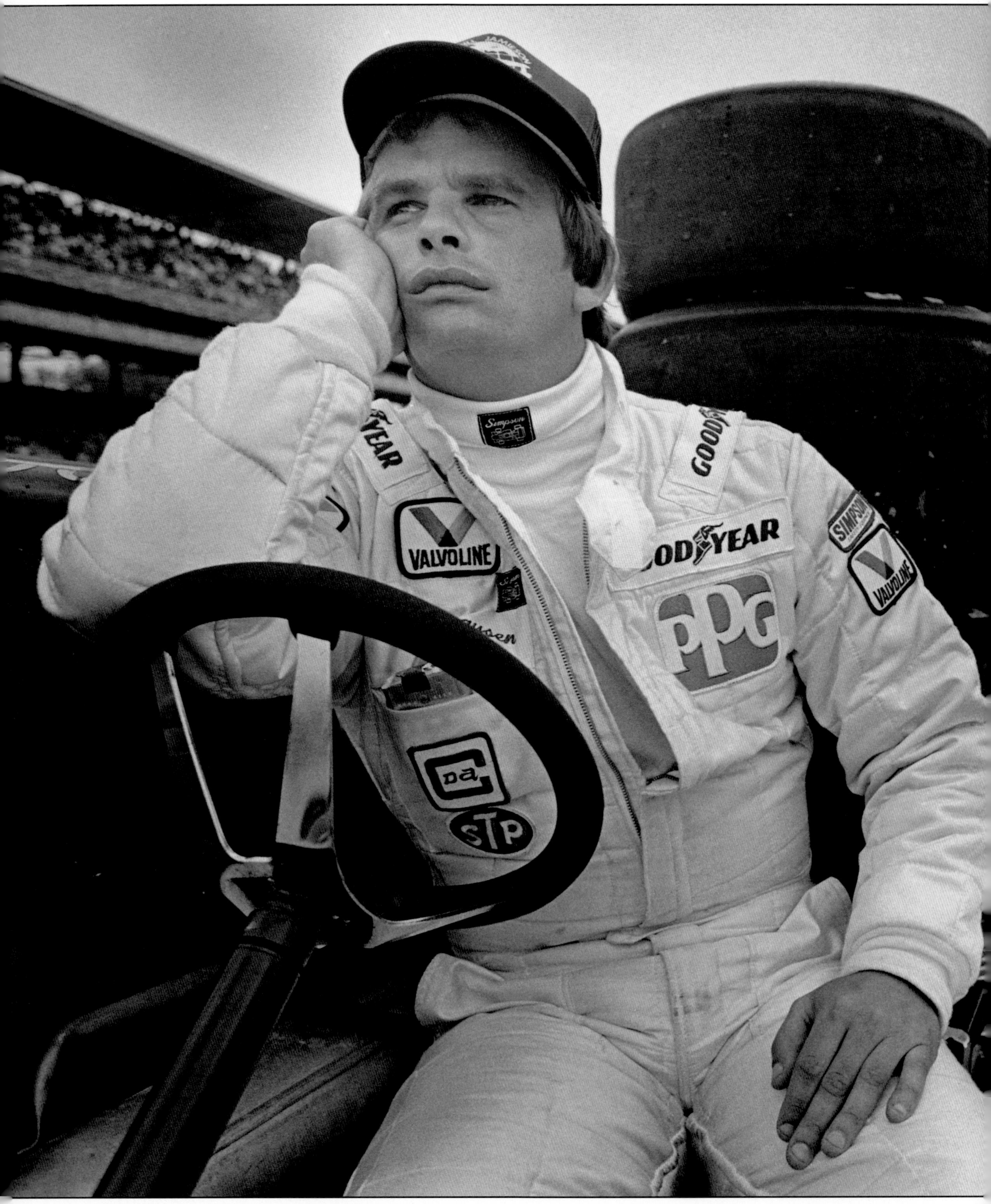
Simpson
VALVOLINE
GOODYEAR
PPG
SIMPSON
VALVOLINE
STP

Spike Gehlhausen, a native of Jasper, missed qualifying for the 1983 Indianapolis 500 by one-quarter inch. That's how far he had to raise the skirt on the left side of his car, and the adjustment cost him six precious miles per hour. The frustration and disappointment etched on his face was three years old; Spike hadn't made the cut since 1980. But in 1984 he was back, and made the field of 33 in the world's Greatest Spectacle in Racing for the fifth time. He took "a quiet retirement" from motorsports in 1988. Today he lives in Indianapolis where he and his brother own and operate a company that manufactures and markets environmental protection products.

ALAN PETERSIME

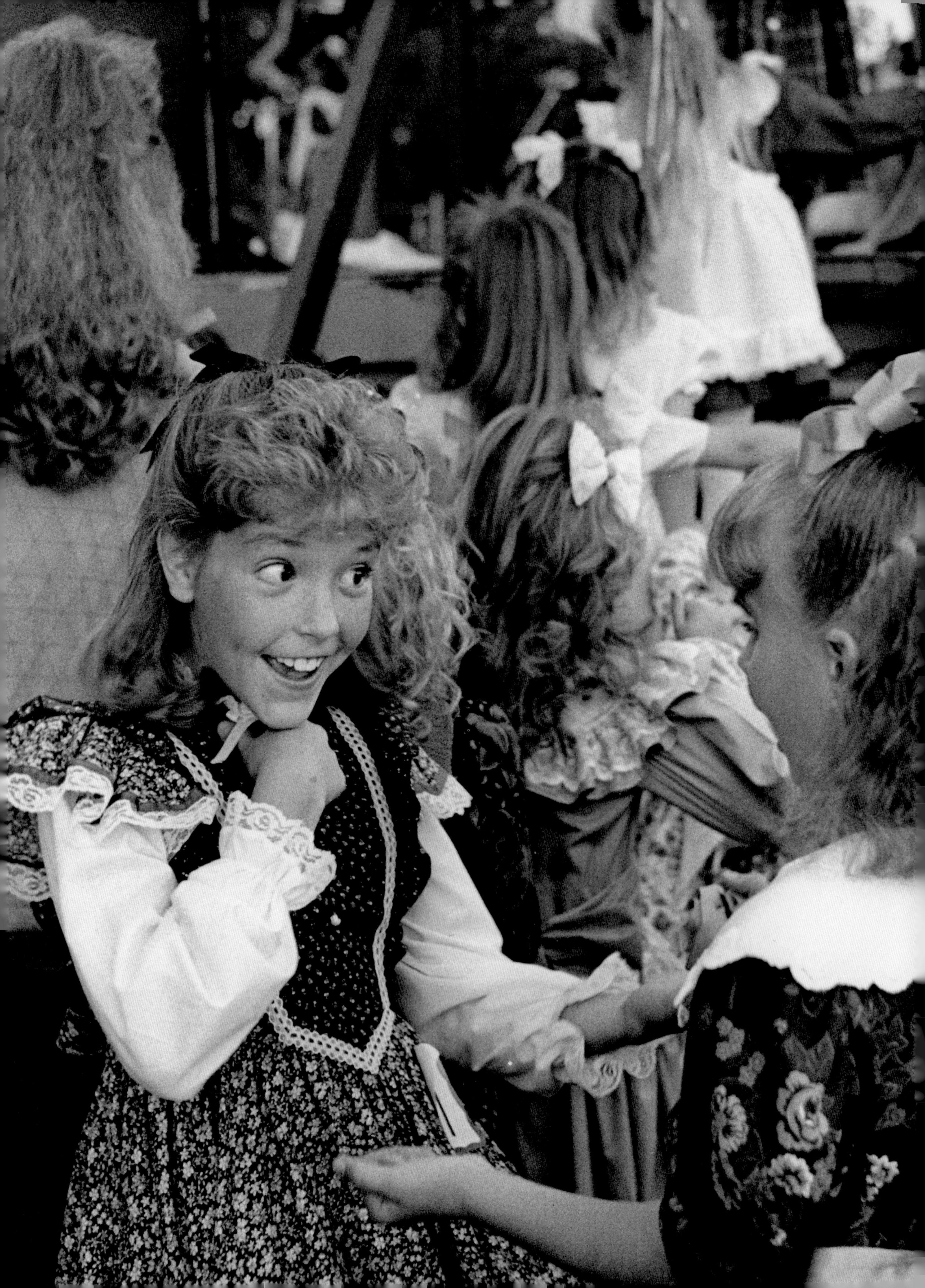

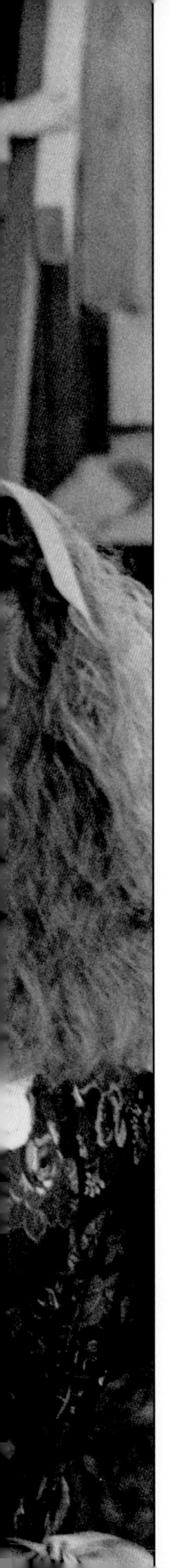

TIM MYERS (Above and left)

Huntingburg focuses on the family during its annual Herbstfest. At left, Jennifer Bertke and Natalie Buening competed in the Little and Junior Miss contest in 1990. Above, Bryan Tanner and Michael Schneider got in a tropical mood while waiting to perform the Beach Boys' "Kokomo" in Puttin' On The Hits in 1994. The zaniest of all fest events, Hits always draws a big crowd. Below, the newly crowned 1986 Herbstfest queen, Mary Henderson, got a congratulatory kiss from her boyfriend, Tom Barnett.

STEVE MELLON

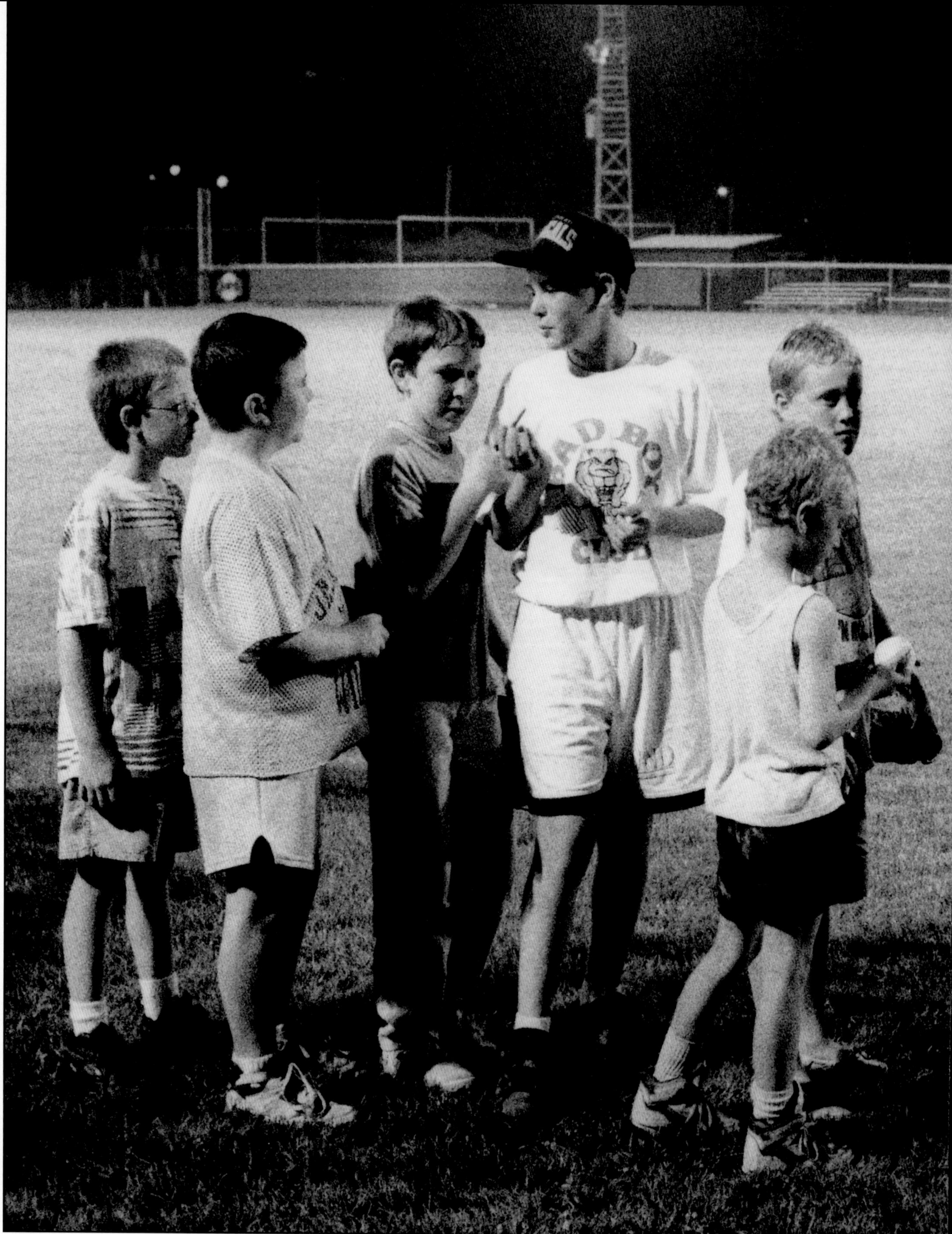

TIM MYERS

*S*cott Rolen, one of the most gifted athletes to come out of Jasper High School, is living every young boy's dream by playing in the Philadelphia Phillies' organization. Rolen also excelled at tennis and basketball. After his last high school game in the 1993 regional, he signed autographs.

Youth sports leagues have long been an integral part of Dubois County life and picture day is always a memorable occasion. Members of the Hawks, a minor league team in the Dubois Girls Softball league, hammed it up for "unofficial" photographer Ron Brosmer in May of 1993. Brosmer has taken team and individual pictures for the league for years.

TIM MYERS

Not all days in front of the camera are joyful. After Jasper High School lost 6-5 in the semi-final game of the 1981 baseball state championship, pitcher Mike Ballenger could not hide his disappointment. The right-hander came into the game toting a streak of 31 scoreless innings. He gave up 11 hits to Fort Wayne Northrop, five of them for extra bases. Ballenger's sports career didn't end with the loss. He won a basketball scholarship at the University of Kentucky, and later transferred to Western Kentucky, where he played ball for the Hilltoppers.

ALAN PETERSIME

ALAN PETERSIME

JEFF TUTTLE

ALAN PETERSIME

Every August since 1979, area residents have dusted off lederhosen and strapped on polka shoes to celebrate their German heritage at the Jasper Strassenfest. The first fest opened with the release of 5,000 helium-filled balloons. Scheduled events included a volleyball tournament, horseshoe pitch and the Wettlauf, a walk/run through city streets. Charles Stenftenagel, president of Stens Corporation, was the first chairman. These days, bands, sports contests, a beer garden and food booths draw thousands from throughout the region, while visitors from Jasper's sister city of Pfaffenweiler, Germany, usually add an element of authenticity to the festivities. The Strassenfest has hosted a variety of events over the years, from the traditional to the weird. The Little Miss contest, above left, has become a staple. In 1983, Dave Wehr acted as official starter for the Barstool Race, above. At left, Kurt Helm and Tommy Englert attended opening ceremonies in traditional dress in 1981.

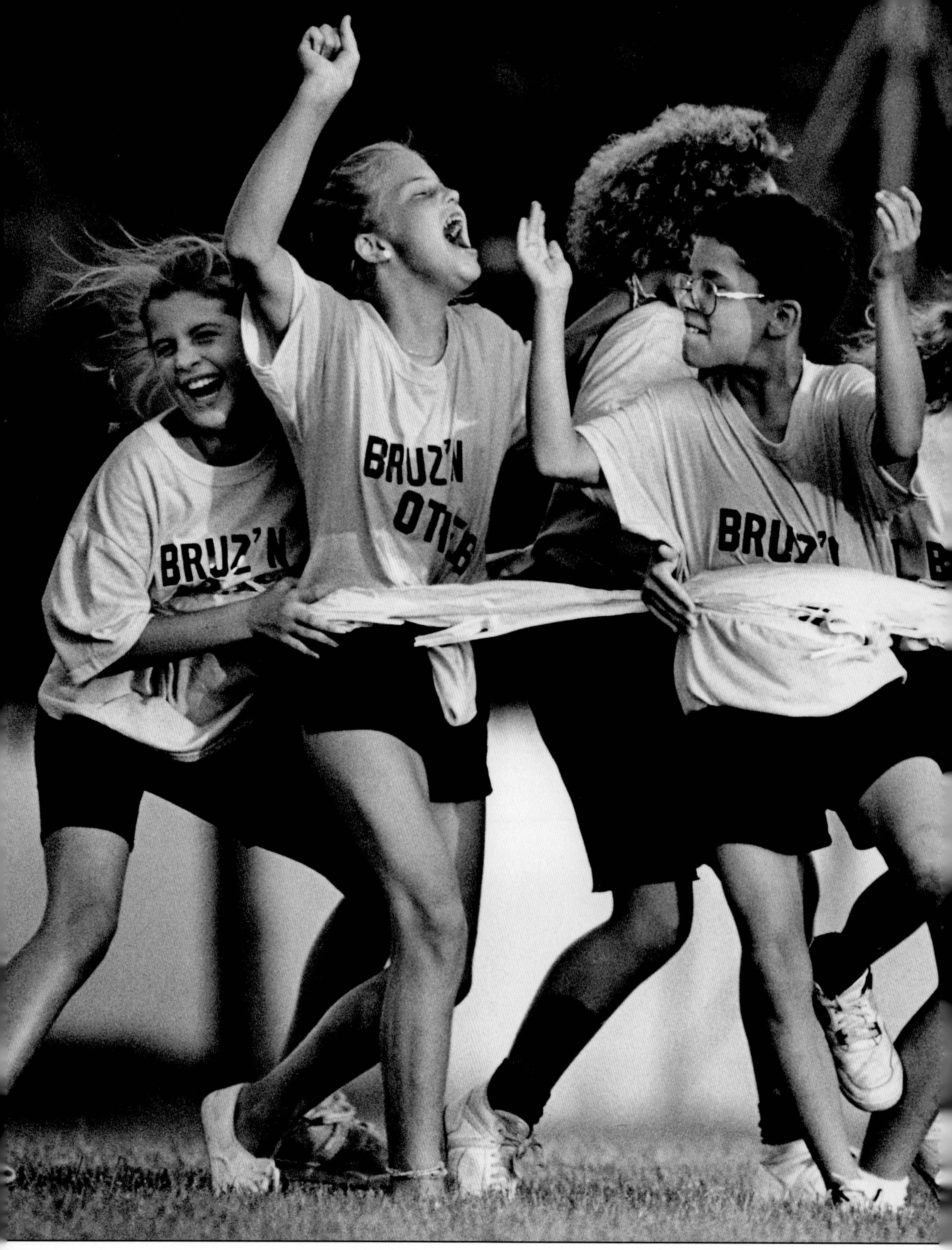
BRUZ'N
BRUZ'N
BRUZ'N

The joy of being young and free in summertime, of running with friends and seeing the finish line just ahead, shows on the faces of Brayden Erny, Klint Heichelbech, Kiersten Hile, Michelle Hopf, Tara Schnaus and Tiffany Small. They were strapped together with an entire roll of masking tape for a race in the Mini Anything Goes contest at Strassenfest in 1989. The six youngsters, members of the Bruz'N Others team, took first place that year.

TIM MYERS

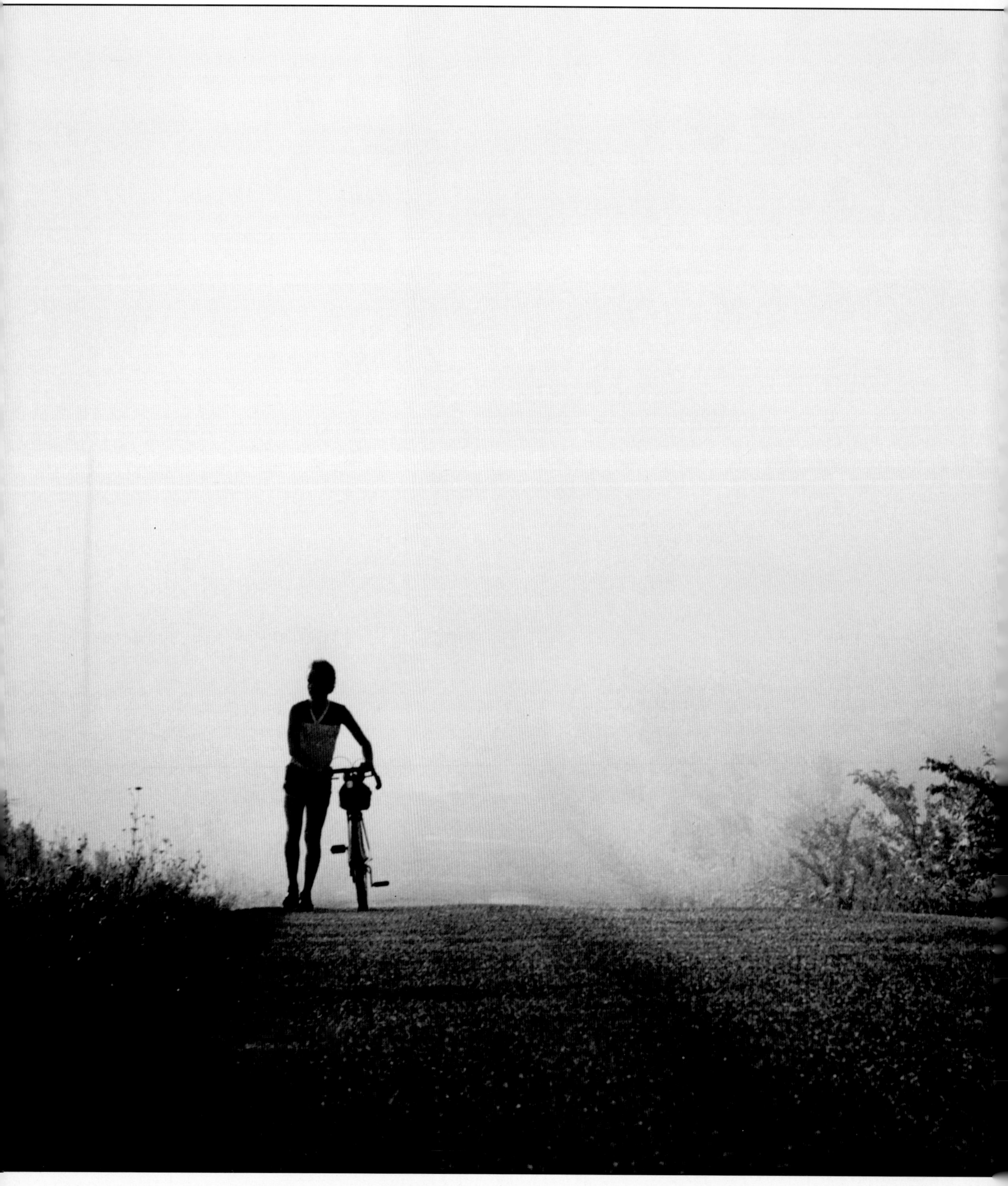

The rolling hills of southern Indiana provide many opportunities for outdoor recreation. Here, early morning fog didn't hinder Daniel Hollinden of St. Henry from touring the backroads near Ferdinand in July of 1986.

STEVE MELLON

ALAN PETERSIME

Acknowledgements

Thanks to the Herald photojournalists, past and present, who contributed to this book.

Tracy L. Albano. Student at Western Kentucky University. Interned at The Herald in summer of 1994.

Torsten Kjellstrand. Interned at The Herald in the summer of 1993. Joined The Herald staff in 1994.

Steve Mellon. Freelance photographer in Pittsburgh. (Herald photographer 1984-87.)

Tim Myers. Joined The Herald in 1989. Currently Chief Photographer.

Mark T. Osler. Freelance photographer in Portland, Ore. (Herald photographer 1993-94.)

Alan Petersime. Picture editor for the Chronicle Tribune in Marion, Ind. (Herald photographer 1978-84.)

John Rumbach. Co-publisher and Editor of The Herald.

Jeff Tuttle. Photographer at the Wichita Eagle-Beacon. (Herald photographer 1987-89.)

Thanks to Herald staff writers and photographers who researched and wrote captions: Cam Bardwell, Hak Haskins, Bill Huddleston, Torsten Kjellstrand, Dave Kunz, Dawn Mazur, Tim Myers, Bill Powell, Michael Rubino and Catherine Senderling.